Amazing Creatures

Coloring Book

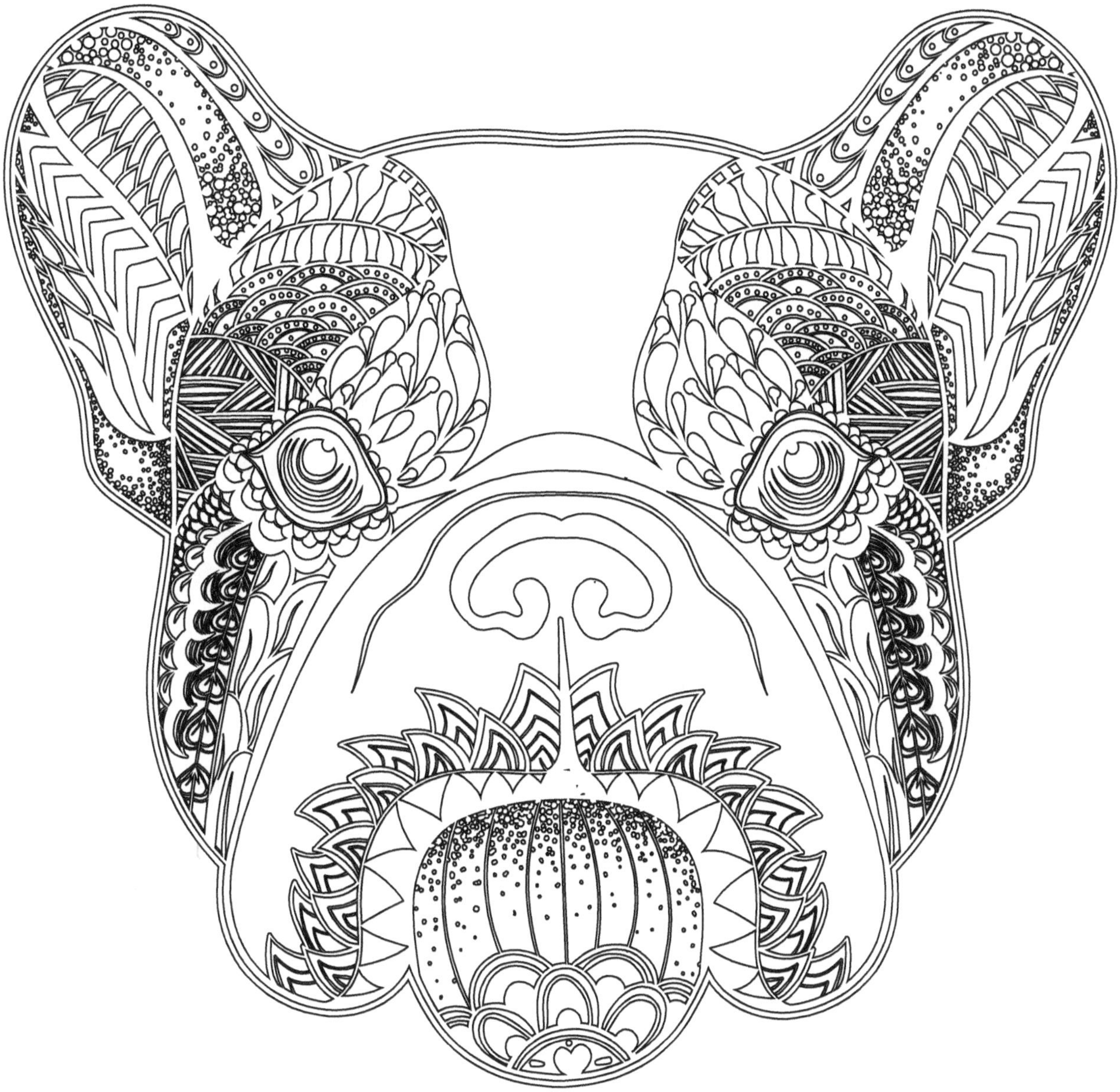

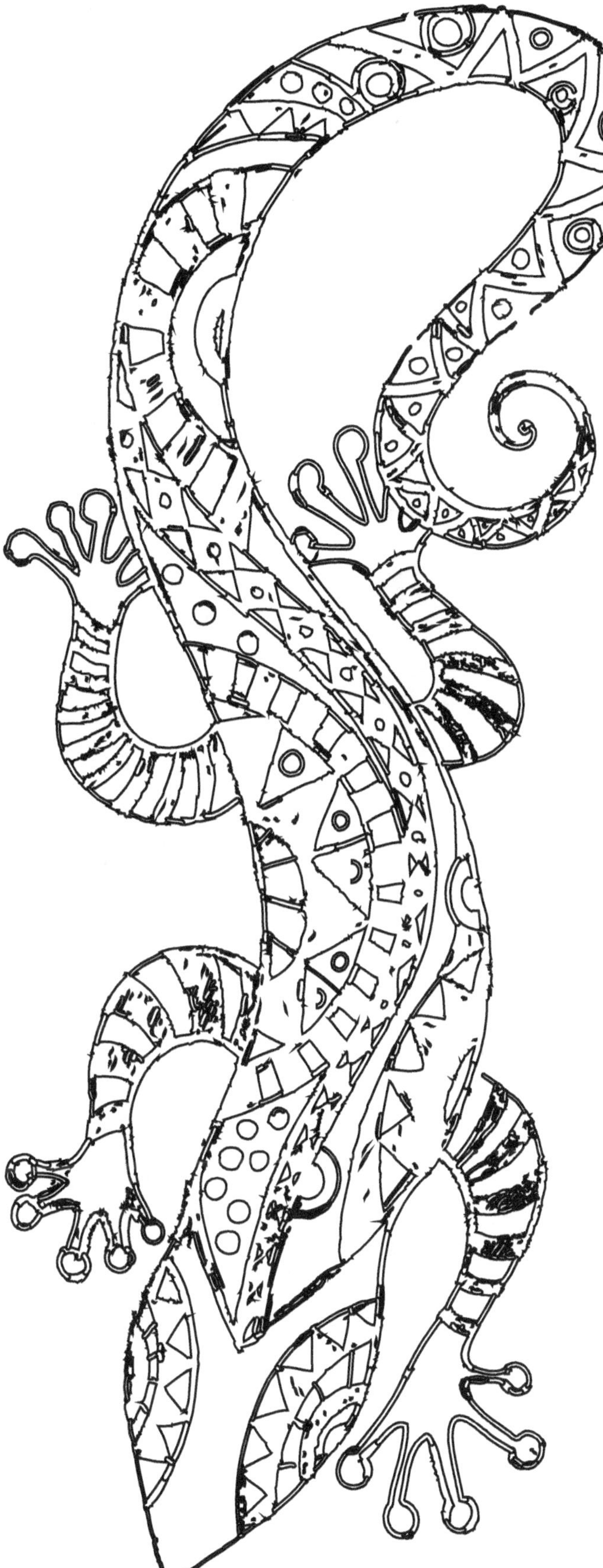

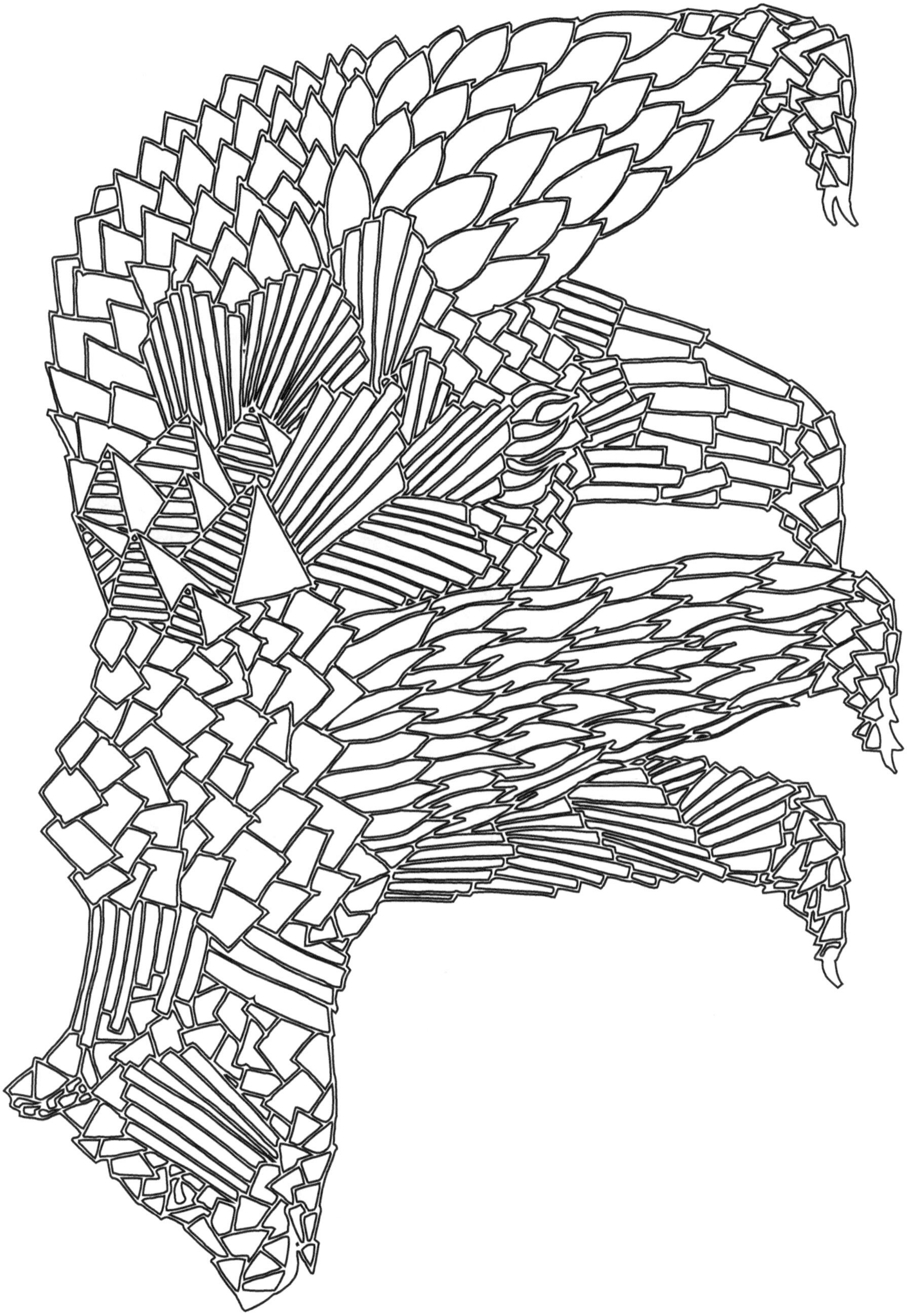

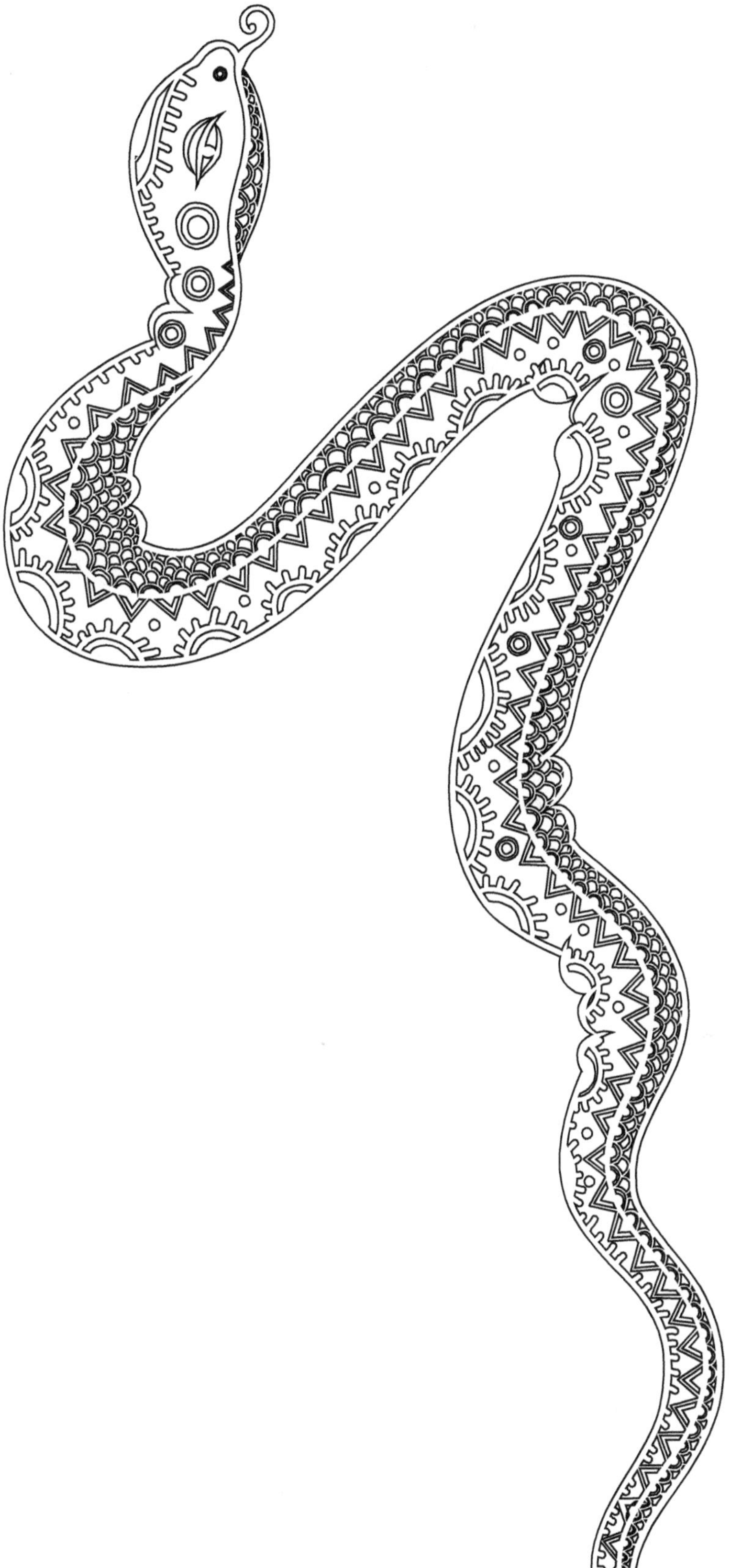

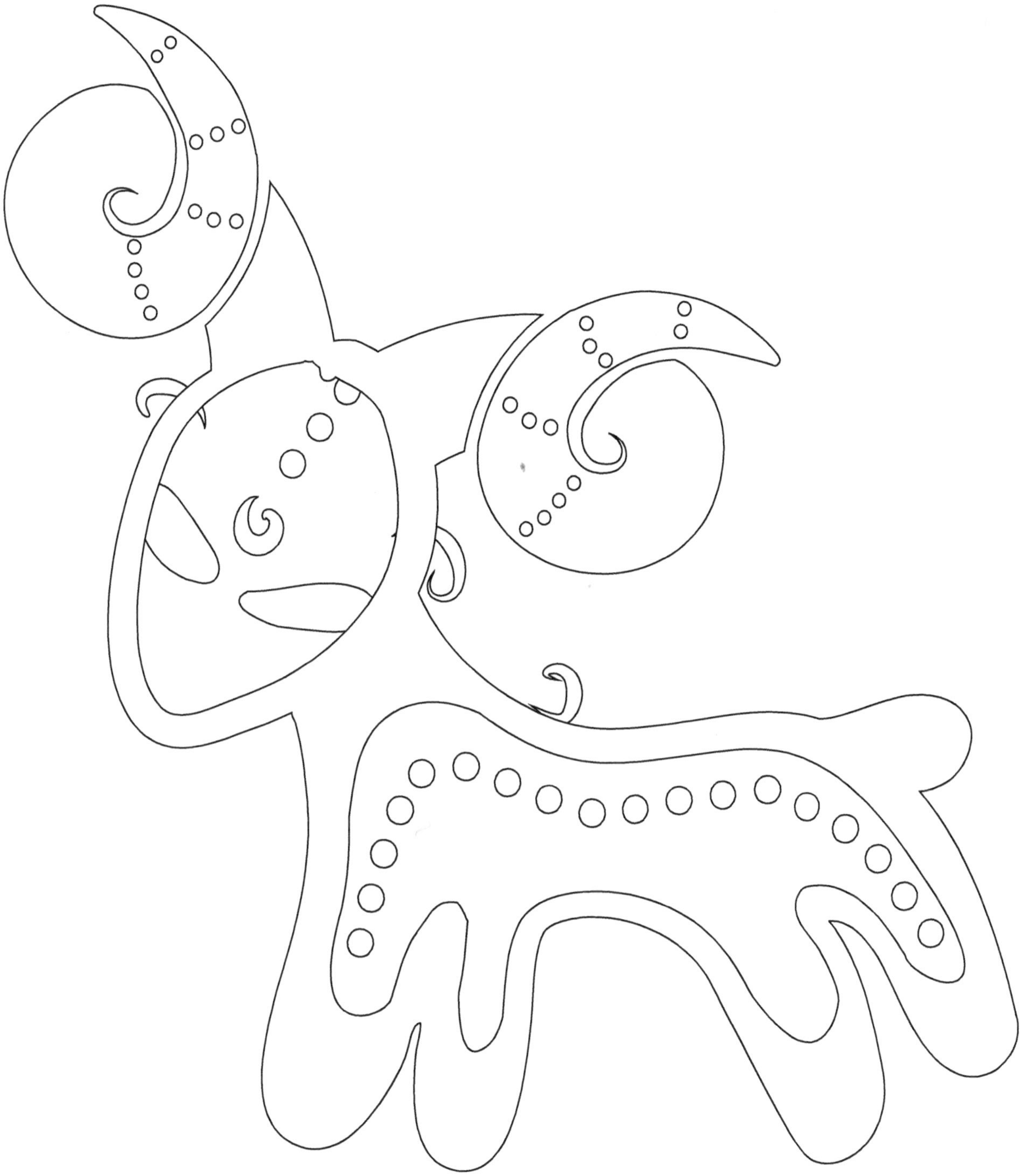

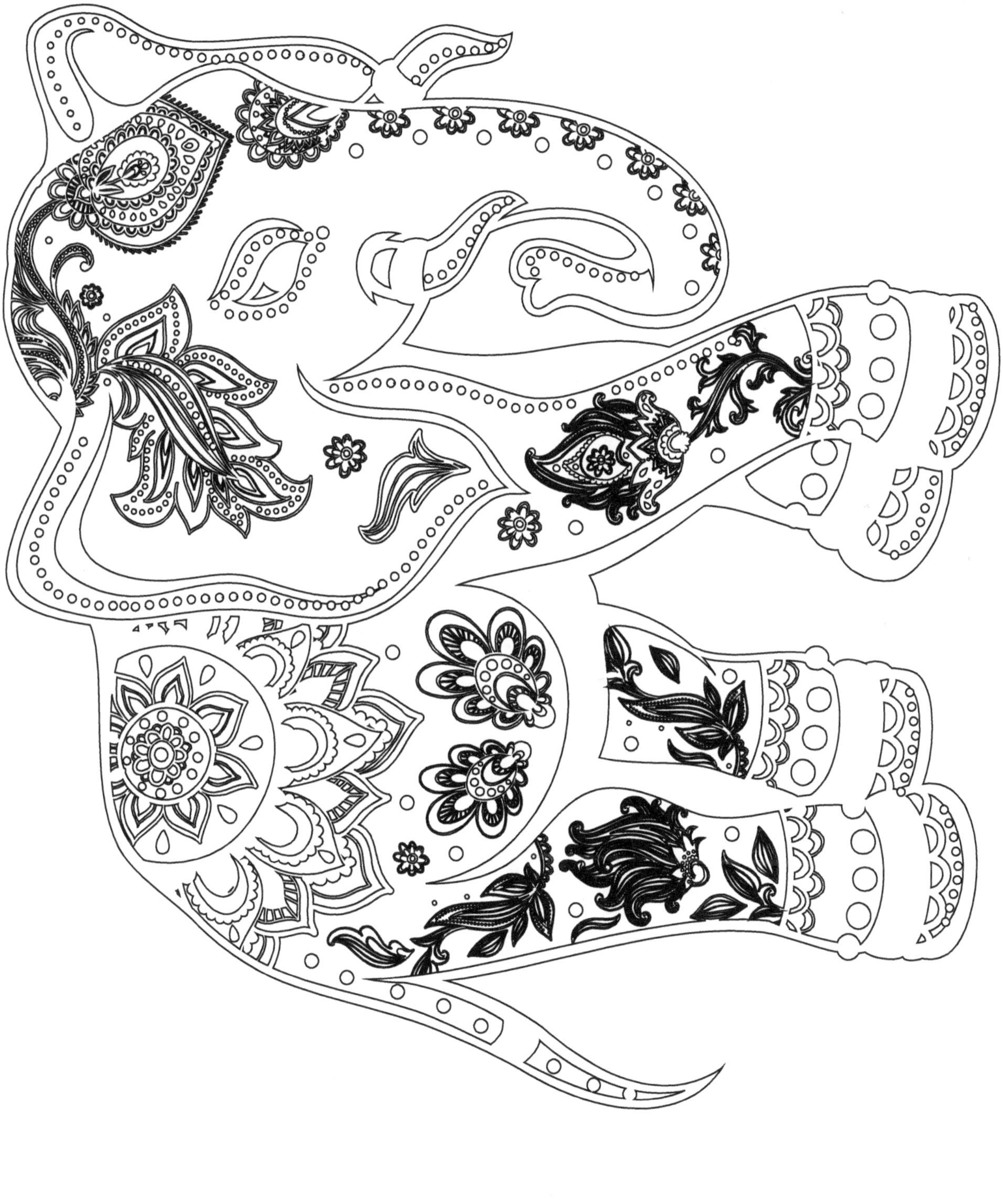

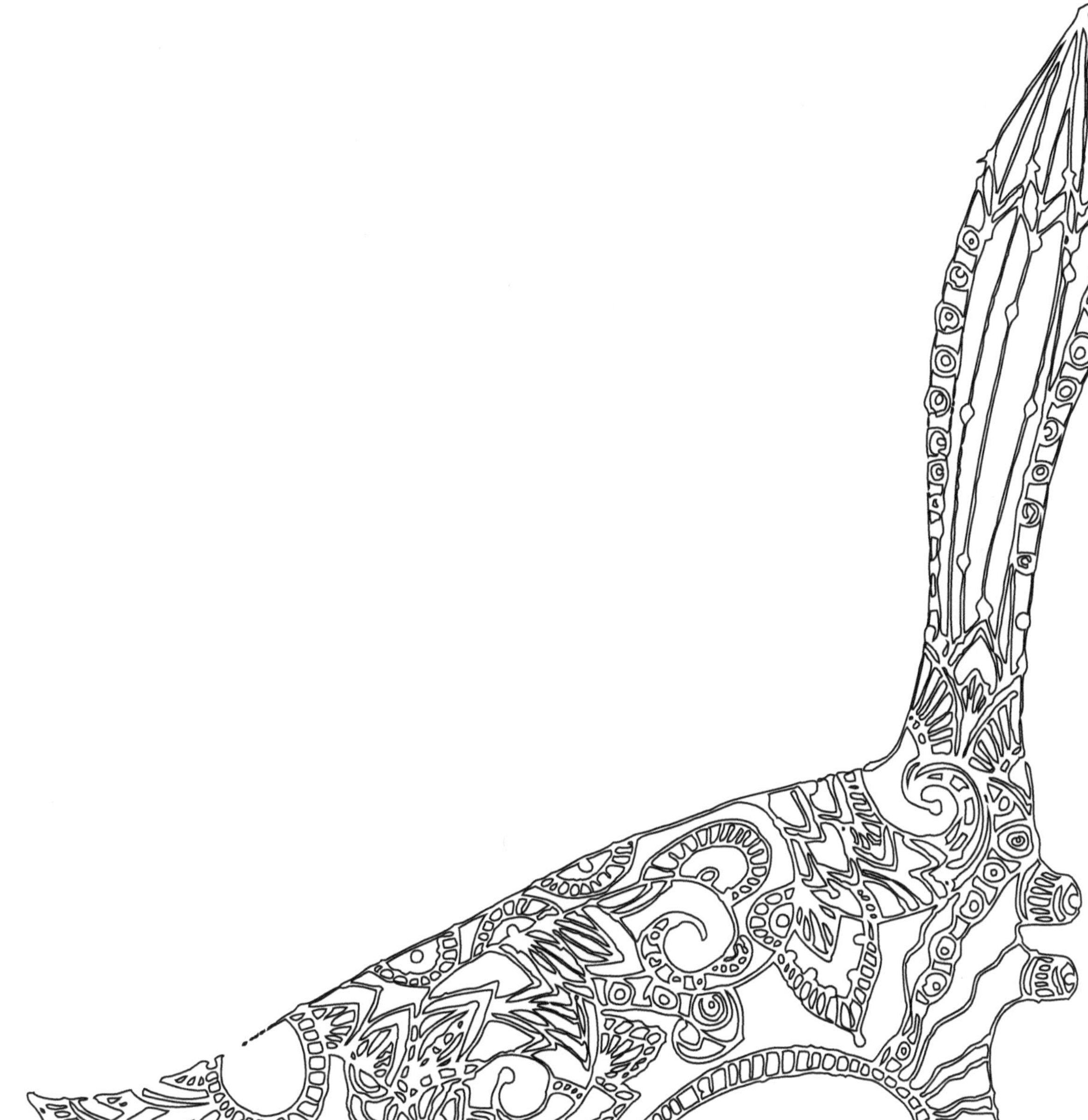

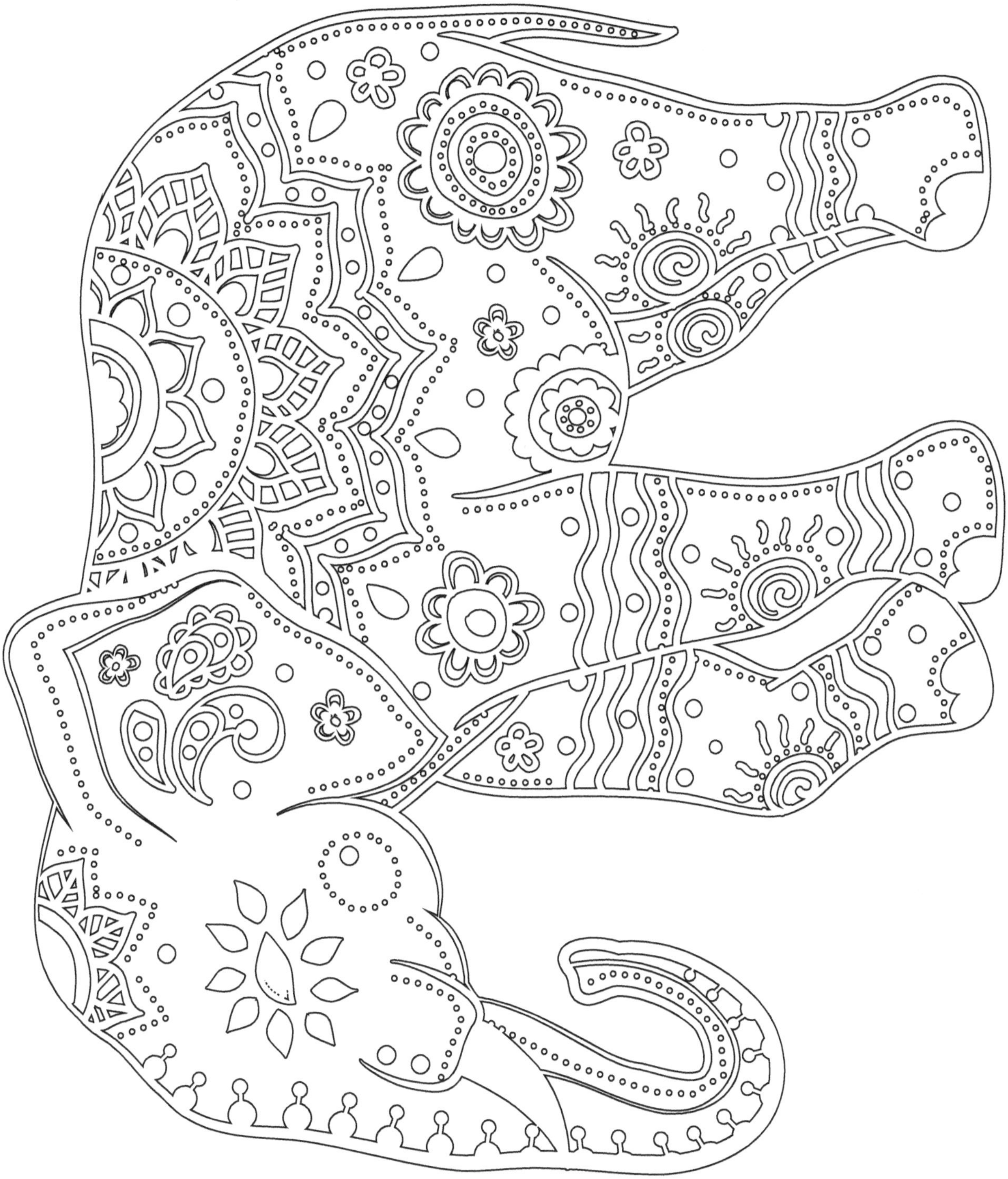

Bonus Pages

To receive more downloadable coloring pages visit

www.coloringbookcorner.com

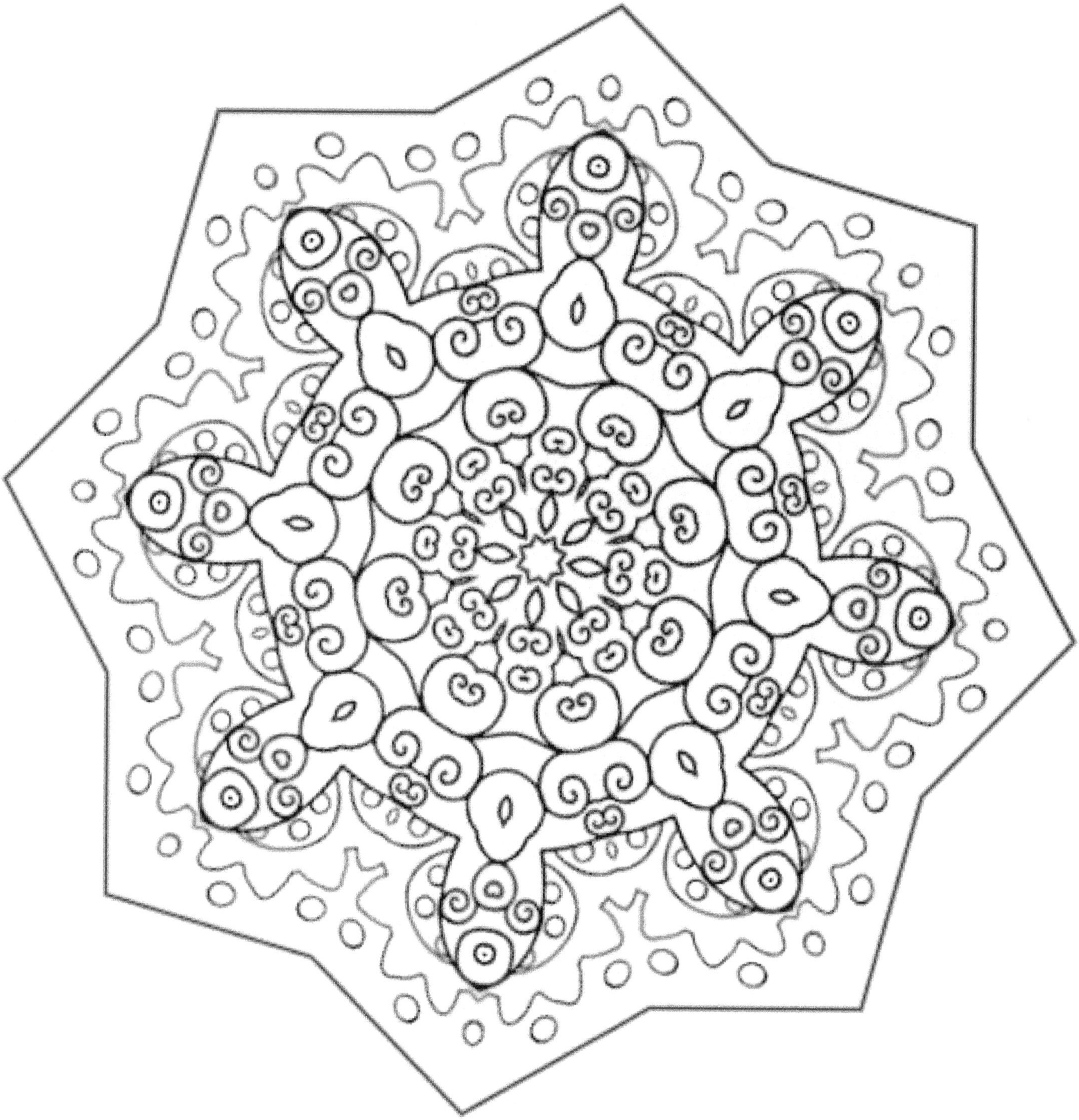

www.ingramcontent.com/pod-product-compliance
Lightning Source LLC
Chambersburg PA
CBHW081149040426
42445CB00015B/1817
* 9 7 8 0 4 7 3 3 4 2 9 4 4 *